What Is Mercy Ministry?

GW00771708

Basics of the Faith

Am I Called?

How Do We Glorify God?

How Our Children Come to Faith

Is Jesus in the Old Testament?

What Are Election and Predestination?

What Are Spiritual Gifts?

What Happens after Death?

What Is a Reformed Church?

What Is a True Calvinist?

What Is Biblical Preaching?

What Is Church Government?

What Is Discipleship?

What Is Faith?

What Is Grace?

What Is Hell?

What Is Justification by Faith Alone?

What Is Man?

What Is Mercy Ministry?

What Is Perseverance of the Saints?

What Is Providence?

What Is Spiritual Warfare?

What Is the Atonement?

What Is the Christian Worldview?

What Is the Doctrine of Adoption?

What Is the Lord's Supper?

What Is the Trinity?

What Is True Conversion?

What Is Vocation?

What Is Worship Music?

Why Believe in God?

Why Do We Baptize Infants?

Why Do We Have Creeds?

Why Do We Pray?

Why God Gave Us a Book

Sean Michael Lucas, Series Editor

What Is Mercy Ministry?

Philip G. Ryken
and Noah J. Toly

P&R
PUBLISHING
P.O. BOX 817 • PHILLIPSBURG • NEW JERSEY 08865-0817

Scripture quotations are from *ESV Bible* ® (*The Holy Bible, English Standard Version* ®). Copyright © 2001 by Crossway Bibles, a publishing ministry of Good News Publishers. Used by permission. All rights reserved.

Italics within Scripture quotations indicate emphasis added.

ISBN: 978-1-59638-518-4 (pbk)
ISBN: 978-1-59638-825-3 (ePub)
ISBN: 978-1-59638-826-0 (Mobi)

Page design by Tobias Design

Printed in the United States of America

Library of Congress Cataloging-in-Publication Data

Ryken, Philip Graham, 1966-
  What is mercy ministry? / Philip G. Ryken and Noah J. Toly.
    p. cm. -- (Basics of the faith)
  Includes bibliographical references.
  ISBN 978-1-59638-518-4 (pbk.)
  1. Mercy. 2. Service (Theology) 3. Church work. I. Toly, Noah. II. Title.
BV4647.M4R95 2013
253--dc23
               2012042483

■ It was disturbing to see the man lying, dirty and disheveled, on the church's doorstep. It was one thing to see homeless people on TV or to drive through the city and view them from the comfort of a warm automobile. But it was another thing to step past a living, breathing, broken-down human being every Sunday morning on the way into church. What was a Christian to do?

This question faced the members of a center-city church one cold, snowy winter in the early 1980s. Times were hard, and Philadelphia's homeless population was growing. By the time church members were stepping over bodies, the problem was too big and too close to ignore.

It would have been easy, of course, to say that these people needed to take responsibility for their own welfare, that they were the victims of their own foolish choices. But who knew for sure? What if they were "more sinn'd against than sinning," to quote a famous line from Shakespeare? Even if they *were* partly to blame for their own poverty, wasn't there something Christians should do to help?

In her poem "Man Sleeping," Jane Kenyon remembers a snowy day in our nation's capital and asks why she still thinks about a man she saw sleeping outside the Sackler Museum. Then she describes the man she saw, lying on top of all his earthly possessions, with his body twisted and his mouth agape. To the poet he looked "like a child who has fallen asleep still dressed on the top of the covers, or like Abel, broken, at his brother's feet."[1]

By mentioning Abel, Kenyon calls to mind the sin of Cain, who murdered his brother and left him to die alone in an open field. She uses this biblical allusion to suggest that someone was responsible for the sorry condition of the man she saw lying on the ground. More pointedly, she helps us to see that, like Cain, we have looked at people in need without taking responsibility for our own fellow creatures or even really caring.

So, what did church members do about the homeless man on their doorstep? They took responsibility for their brother, offering him food and clothing. But this was only the beginning. The deacons empowered and motivated church members to respond in faith and obedience. Seeking to put biblical principles into practice and believing that the gospel called them to compassion, they met regularly for prayer, asking God to show them which ministries of mercy he wanted them to start. Soon they established a food pantry, a clothing closet, and a weekly dinner for their homeless neighbors.

Although this story of everyday compassion took place in the City of Brotherly Love, it could have happened anywhere— in any city, village, or suburban community in the world. Mercy ministry always begins with the recognition of profound human need. Mercy is then offered in gratitude to God for the grace he has given in Jesus Christ and out of a genuine desire to imitate his love.

Mercy ministry usually starts in the hearts of people who are not very experienced in meeting other people's needs and who may in fact find it hard to love other people. Yet they are aware of the suffering around them and open to serving God in whatever way he wants them to serve. In other words, mercy ministry usually begins with someone like you: an ordinary sinner saved by grace who is willing to be useful for the kingdom of God by caring for somebody else in need.

THE NEED FOR MERCY MINISTRY

What kind of world is it where some find themselves with shelter and others go without? What accounts for our profound needs and the suffering of those around us?

As Scripture attests, we live in a world marked by frustration, decay, and pain. Because of sin,

> the creation was subjected to futility, not willingly, but because of him who subjected it, in hope that the creation itself will be set free from its bondage to corruption and obtain the freedom of the glory of the children of God. For we know that the whole creation has been groaning together in the pains of childbirth until now. (Rom. 8:20–22)

Paul's vivid images of futility, corruption, and agony capture the turmoil of a world marked by both ordinary and spectacular instances of suffering.

Because suffering originates with evil, it is helpful to distinguish between *natural* and *moral* evil. As Daniel Migliore defines the term, "Natural evil refers to injury and suffering caused by diseases, accidents, earthquakes, fires, and floods." When we imagine suffering arising from natural evil, we might consider people born with a crippling disease or deformity or "think of a young mother mortally stricken by cancer . . . of thousands buried in a mudslide caused by a volcanic eruption, of hundreds killed in a plane crash in a dense fog."[2]

While some natural suffering goes unnoticed for years or is known only to a few people, other suffering makes headlines. Events from the early years of the twenty-first century have seared our memories with images of natural evil and the suffering that results. From the 2004 Indian Ocean tsunami that destroyed communities in fourteen countries and claimed the lives of more than 230,000 people, to Hurricane Katrina that devastated New Orleans, to the 2010 Haiti earthquake that created millions of homeless and orphans in a matter of moments, to Japan's 2011 earthquake, tsunami, and nuclear crisis, we are frequently reminded that the world is not the way it's supposed to be.

News of catastrophic natural disasters travels quickly and widely, but their consequences can linger for generations after media coverage subsides. Each of the above instances was marked by the subsequent outbreak of disease—often because of compromised water resources for drinking, cooking, cleaning, and bathing. These "circumstantial calamities" cause lasting poverty and profound suffering.[3]

In contrast to natural evil, moral evil is characterized by injustice and oppression, willful negligence, and personal failure. In order to describe moral evil, Migliore contrasts the eighteenth century's primary symbol of suffering, the Lisbon earthquake of 1755, with the twentieth century's primary symbol of suffering, the Holocaust.[4] In recent decades, the Holocaust has been joined by the Rwandan genocide, the Balkan crisis, 9/11, and the War on Terror as symbols of suffering caused by moral evil.

Yet not all such suffering is caused by evil intentions of historic proportions. Suffering can emerge from structures that we take for granted, such as social systems that protect the privileged while marginalizing racial, ethnic, or religious minorities, women, or the poor. Suffering is also caused by willfully negligent or intentional evil, such as an abusive spouse or parent or a small business owner who withholds wages from his employees. We can think of the lawless trade in illegal drugs and arms in northern Mexico and the attendant unprecedented violence that has limited economic opportunity for those who would pursue lawful employment. We may recall infamous school massacres—Columbine, Virginia Tech, Northern Illinois University—or a mass murder in Tucson, Arizona, that claimed the life of a nine-year-old girl at a political rally. We might consider the case of poor communities that endure the effects of toxic waste illegally dumped in their neighborhoods. We should remind ourselves as well of the tens of millions of abortions performed since 1973 in the United States alone.

In these examples, suffering originates with the evil of others, yet some suffering originates with the sin of the sufferer. A pornography addict, for example, not only risks the suffering of friends and family but also his or her own spiritual and psychological turmoil.[5] Not only earthquakes, tidal waves, and pogroms but also laziness, folly, fraud, and sinful indulgence can result in poverty and homelessness. As Scripture makes clear, people reap the temporal harvest of their own sin (e.g., Prov. 1:20–33).

In order to understand our calling in a world marked by these consequences of evil—from poverty and homelessness to natural disasters and genocide—we must consider the origins of evil. Suffering caused by moral evil is a result of contemporary sin, yet it has its roots in the first sin recorded in Genesis 3. Scripture teaches not only that the *wages* of the first sin are borne by all humanity—as Romans 5 declares—

but also that *sinfulness* itself has been passed down across generations to all humanity. As the Westminster Confession of Faith teaches, all actual transgressions proceed from the original corruption of Adam and Eve, "whereby we are utterly indisposed, disabled, and made opposite to all good, and wholly inclined to all evil."[6]

Natural evil is also a result of the fall; specifically, it is a consequence of the curse spoken by God in Genesis 3:14–19. The first sin resulted not only in persistent alienation between God and human beings, and between human beings and other human beings, but also between humans and the non-human created order. Because of our failure to be what we were meant to be, God has subjected creation to frustration, decay, and pain.

But Paul teaches in Romans 8:23 that as creation waits and groans with us, testifying to suffering and need, it eagerly anticipates the revelation of God's adopted children and the healing that will accompany that revelation. God pledges to end the frustration, decay, and pain that we all experience.

How will God do this? And what should we do about suffering in the meantime? What is our role in a world marked by suffering and hardship? What motivates God's people to work toward the alleviation of suffering while eagerly awaiting and fervently desiring the cosmic restoration that God promises?

A THEOLOGY FOR MERCY MINISTRY

Some years ago now, a team of sociologists visited a center-city church. They were conducting a study of congregations involved in mercy ministry. When they had finished their report, they gave the pastors a chance to read through it to check for mistakes before publication.

Although the report was well written, there was one sentence the pastors found hard to accept. It went something like this: "Although this church is deeply committed to teaching and preaching biblical doctrine, it also has a heart for mercy ministry." The pastors told the researchers, "All you have to do is change one word and we'll be satisfied. Take the word 'although' and change it to 'because.'" Upon further reflection, the researchers agreed to make the change, so the final version of their report read, "*Because* this church is deeply committed to teaching and preaching biblical doctrine, it has a heart for mercy ministry." Words of gospel truth compel deeds of gospel mercy. Far from being hindered by an emphasis on theology, the ministry of mercy is fueled by Christian doctrine, properly understood.

So what does our theology say about mercy? Often when people talk about the theology of mercy ministry, they start with *the doctrine of the incarnation*. Effective mercy ministry is incarnational, they say: it meets people where they are. When we meet people where they are—showing them mercy in their time of need—we are simply imitating God the Son incarnate, who came down from heaven's throne to Bethlehem's manger, took on the flesh of our humanity, and had mercy on our lost and fallen race. Now the Savior who gave up his riches to get us out of our desperate spiritual poverty (2 Cor. 8:9) calls us to use our riches to care for the poor.

All this is true. But the theological basis for mercy ministry is both broader, encompassing a fuller array of doctrines, and deeper, beginning much further back than the incarnation.

Perhaps it is best to begin with *the doctrine of God* and to consider all the divine attributes that compel us to show mercy. There is mercy itself, for God is "rich in mercy" (Eph. 2:4). Then there are the attributes that are closely related to mercy: compassion, kindness, and love. And what about attributes like patience and longsuffering? These divine attributes define the mercy God shows to us, and thus they ought to characterize the mercy we show to others. Nor should we forget justice, because showing mercy to the needy often involves defending the righteousness of their cause. Such justice flows from the character of God, because our God is just (see Ex. 34:6–7).

These virtues are demanded whenever we show mercy, and they all find their source in the character of God. Furthermore, all these attributes are characteristic of each Person of the Trinity. The Father is the God of all comfort; the Son is the God of perfect love; the Spirit is the God of sweet compassion.

Thus, mercy ministry is a reflection of the being and the nature of the Triune God. The German theologian Ulrich Bach spoke with profound insight when he said: "Tell me how you talk about God and I will tell you what your [mercy ministry] is like, or what handicapped people can expect from you, or whether you expect anything from them."[7]

The doctrine of God is only the beginning. Next we consider the doctrine of election. What does this deep mystery teach us about showing mercy? It teaches us that people are never saved by their own merit but only by the sovereign grace of God, who has mercy on whom he has mercy (Rom. 9:15). This humbles our pride and teaches us to love people who seem to be undeserving, for so are we. The doctrine of election also reminds us that our call to show mercy is older than time itself: every act of mercy is one of the "good works, which God prepared beforehand, that we should walk in them" (Eph. 2:10).

After election, we consider *the doctrine of creation*, which teaches that the one true God made the entire universe out of nothing. This is the part of our theology that declares the goodness of God's world and reminds us of the way things are supposed to be. It is also the doctrine that declares to us the dignity of the people God made in his image (see Gen. 1:27)—the dignity that gives them a claim on our mercy. Every human being who has ever lived shares equally in this divine image: old and young; born and unborn; able and disabled; rich and poor; uptown and downtown; from the right side of the tracks and the wrong side of the tracks; my color and your color. Each of us is made in the image of a merciful God.

Without the doctrine of the image of God, we would always be tempted to divide people into two groups: the people who deserve our mercy and the people who don't. John Freeman confronted this way of thinking in one of his ministry newsletters for Harvest USA by recounting the time he met a homeless man outside a corner grocery store. "Can you spare a quarter, mister?" the man said. Freeman turned him down and went inside, but the man was still there when he came back out. "Can you spare a quarter?" When Freeman hesitated, the man said, "Son, come a little closer." So he came closer, close enough to smell the man's stench of sweat and dirt and alcohol. Suddenly, the man reached out, placed his hand on Freeman's shoulder, and said, "Son, I haven't always been out here on the streets, you know. I was somebody once."[8]

Our theology begs to differ. According to the doctrine of creation, there is no such thing as somebody who *was* somebody but isn't somebody anymore. Everybody is somebody—somebody made in the image of a merciful God. When we see his image in ourselves, we know that we are called to be like God in showing mercy to people in need. And when we recognize his image in others, we know that we are supposed to offer them the same mercy that we have received. This explains why John Calvin believed that caring for the poor was as sacred as the worship of God, that *pietas* and *caritas*—the duties of worship and love—were inseparable.[9] He knew that the people we serve are made in the image of God. Thus, in serving them we give honor to God.

What other doctrines help to provide a theological basis for mercy ministry? As we have seen, the doctrine of depravity explains why mercy is needed. But the Bible also teaches *the doctrine of redemption*, which explains how mercy is made possible. God is at work in the world to bring salvation, specifically through the person and work of Jesus Christ. "Blessed be the God and Father of our Lord Jesus Christ! According to his *great mercy*, he has caused us to be born again to a living hope through . . . Jesus Christ" (1 Peter 1:3).

Everything about the reconciling ministry of Jesus Christ teaches us to show mercy. First Jesus became one of us to save us. Now, as the Father sent us the Son, Jesus sends us out into the world (see John 20:21), where our ministry of servant mercy incarnates his grace. Just as he visited us in our distress, so we are called "to visit orphans and widows in their affliction" (James 1:27).

In showing mercy, we follow the pattern that Jesus set for us in his own ministry. Our Savior showed mercy with his words. Whatever he said—whether it was a word of warning to the proud, comfort to the suffering, or instruction to the ignorant—Jesus was offering mercy to whoever listened. He also showed mercy with his actions. With every miracle he performed—every time he gave sight to the blind, mobility to the lame, hearing to the deaf, or life to the dead—Jesus was offering mercy to the people whose lives he touched.

In word as well as in deed, his ministry of proclaiming the gospel and healing a groaning creation serves as our model. Our own words of grace and deeds of mercy bear witness to the gospel of Jesus, signifying the coming of the kingdom of God.

Having been shaped by the life of Christ in his earthly work, our ministry of mercy is also marked by his death. An authentic theology of mercy is always a theology of the cross. At the cross we find the atoning mercy of our own forgiveness, which only comes by a perfect sacrifice suffered to the very death. The mercy of the crucified Christ sets the agenda for our own ministry. Just as Jesus laid down his life for us, so we also lay down our lives for others (see 1 John 3:16). God had mercy on us in Christ; now, through us, he wants to show his mercy to others.

The gospel is not just the cross, however; it is also the empty tomb. So our theology of mercy goes beyond the death of Christ to his life beyond the grave and his resurrection work of cosmic restoration. In the midst of the hard struggle of life in a suffering world, the empty tomb gives us the hope of new life and a new creation. The same power that raised Jesus from the dead is now at work in us to make us more merciful. It is also at work in others, including all the desperate, almost hopeless cases we meet. Whether it is the heroin addict on the street corner or the woman whose husband left her for another woman (or man), we all have our own stories to tell of people who seem to be beyond any help. How will they receive mercy? Only by the life of the empty tomb, which is as much a mercy to us as the bloody cross.

Remember as well that the risen Christ is also the ascended Christ, who now sits at the right hand of God, praying for us to receive mercy (Rom. 8:34; Heb. 7:25). We should never stop at the cross when we think about Christ-centered ministry; we should always rise from the empty tomb to the throne of heaven, where our merciful Savior reigns in glory. In ascending to heaven, Jesus has sent down the Spirit, who has poured out on us all the gifts that we need to show people mercy in word and deed.

Part of the Spirit's work is to take the benefits of salvation—all the blessings that flow to us on the basis of the crucifixion, resurrection, and ascension of the Son of God—and apply them to us. As the Spirit gives us these blessings, he calls us again and again to show mercy.

We see the Spirit's call to mercy in our justification by grace alone—or perhaps we should say: *mercy* alone. According to *the doctrine of justification*, we are not accepted by God through works of our own righteousness; rather, by the mercy of God, we are covered with the righteousness of Jesus Christ. This is the hope we offer to all the messed-up, tired-out, broken-down people we meet in ministry: there is hope for people like them (and like us) in Jesus.

Next we move to *the doctrine of adoption*, which assures us that we really are the children of God. If we are sons and daughters of God through faith in Jesus Christ, then we are called to live up to our family likeness. And if there is one thing we know about the head of our household, it is that he is the "Father of the fatherless and protector of widows" (Ps. 68:5). Knowing this, there is a longing in our hearts for all the lost children to enter our Father's house. So in mercy we go to them; with words of truth and deeds of love, we hand them their adoption papers, inviting them home to God.

We continue with *the doctrine of sanctification* (which shows how mercy changes lives from the inside out), *the doctrine of perseverance* (which teaches that mercy never gives up), and *the doctrine of glorification* (which shows how beautiful people become when God finishes the merciful work that he starts). Then we consider *the doctrine of the church*, which teaches us not to do all the ministry on our own (though some of us have tried), but to offer mercy as a community, using whatever gifts God has given to us as part of a larger, cooperative effort, a practical way to implement our confession that we believe in "the communion of saints."

Lastly, the call of mercy comes to us in our *doctrine of the final judgment*. What will Jesus say on the last of all days, when every person who has ever lived is poised between heaven and hell? To everyone who loves justice and shows mercy he will say,

> Come, you who are blessed by my Father, inherit the kingdom prepared for you from the foundation of the world. For I was hungry and you gave me food, I was thirsty and you gave me drink, I was a stranger and you welcomed me, I was naked and you clothed me, I was sick and you visited me, I was in prison and you came to me. . . . Truly, I say to you, as you did it to one of the least of these my brothers, you did it to me. (Matt. 25:34–36, 40)

In short, it is not this part or that part of our theology that compels us to show mercy. Rather, it is everything in the whole system of Christian doctrine: God and man, creation and redemption, sin and salvation. Every doctrine that is taught in every part of Scripture—everything from election to the final judgment—compels us to show the Father's mercy to lost sinners, in the gospel of his Son, by the power of the Holy Spirit.

THE LEGACY OF MERCY MINISTRY

The people of God have always been called to the work of mercy ministry, which is not only commended, but also commanded, throughout Scripture. In the Old Testament, God is frequently described as "merciful and gracious, slow to anger and abounding in steadfast love" (Ps. 103:8). This is how God's old covenant people knew their God: as a God of mercy and grace. Even Jonah, who was dissatisfied with God's mercy toward Nineveh, had to admit: "You are a gracious God and merciful, slow to anger and abounding in steadfast love, and relenting from disaster" (Jonah 4:2).

This merciful God commands his people to be like him, to be set apart from others not only through liturgy but also through mercy. He desires mercy, not sacrifice (Matt. 9:13; cf. Hos. 6:6). As he said through his prophet Micah, "Will the LORD be pleased with thousands of rams, with ten thousands of rivers of oil? . . . He has told you, O man, what is good; and what does the LORD require of you but to do justice, and to love kindness, and to walk humbly with your God?" (Mic. 6:7–8).

This demand for a just mercy is often directed toward the powerful and the wealthy. As Daniel exhorted Nebuchadnezzar, "Break off your sins by practicing righteousness and your iniquities by showing mercy to the oppressed" (Dan. 4:27). But the prophets called all of God's people to mercy: "Learn to do good," Isaiah prophesied; "seek justice, correct oppression; bring justice to the fatherless and plead the widow's cause" (Isa. 1:17).

When Jesus came to fulfill the law (Matt. 5:17), he commended, commanded, and demonstrated mercy. And when the church, in the power of the Holy Spirit, continued this ministry after the ascension, the apostles found it fitting to establish an office specifically devoted to caring for the poor, ordaining Stephen, Philip, and five others for this purpose (Acts 6). In the new covenant, a merciful God sets apart his people for mercy.

The early church fulfilled this calling. The Roman Emperor Julian saw that Christianity was growing due to its ministry of mercy. Christianity, he noted, "has been specially advanced through the loving service rendered to strangers. . . . The [Christians] care not only for their own poor but for ours as well; while those who belong to us look in vain for the help that we should render them."[10] Evidently the words and deeds of the church fathers had shaped a merciful church. In 366, Basil of Caesarea directed the construction of a leprosarium to care for the sick; there Gregory of Nazianzus preached his famous sermon, "On Love for the Poor." Addressed to "brothers and fellow paupers—for we are all poor and needy where divine grace is concerned"—his sermon exhorted believers to gain their lives "by acts of charity," to "appropriate the beatitude that blesses those who are merciful," and to visit, heal, feed, clothe, welcome, and honor Christ by doing the same to the poor and vulnerable.[11]

Later, the plight of the poor served as an instigating concern of the Protestant Reformation, as evidenced by Luther's Ninety-Five Theses, many of which relate to the social situation of the most vulnerable. As part of this broader Protestant movement, the Reformed tradition has emphasized the importance of mercy ministry. From Calvin's Geneva to Thomas Chalmers's ministry in Glasgow to contemporary ministries in global cities and other sites around the world, the rich theological resources of the Reformation have motivated merciful engagement with a suffering world. As we pursue faithful ministry in the midst of hardship and turmoil, each of these examples has something to teach us about serving the marginalized and vulnerable in our own context.

Calvin's Geneva

In 1536, the French Reformer John Calvin was called to shepherd the church in Geneva, Switzerland. We should not mistake the city for an idyllic setting in which needs were few and burdens were light. One Reformation historian describes the squalor of Calvin's Geneva:

> Like most middling cities of the 16th century, Geneva's foetid physical space was small, and its inhabitants rubbed shoulders daily in social interactions and commerce. Such was the age. It is recounted that when the humanist Erasmus passed through the squares of Basel he would cover his nose with a cloth on account of the stench. In narrow streets, churches, market places and taverns, friends and enemies were in constant contact, knowing nothing of our modern sense of privacy. Rumour and gossip were the daily fare of social discourse, and violence a common means of conflict resolution. . . . All across Europe rulers and common people worried about what to do with the youth, in particular young men, the poor and foreigners. Fear of disease and the threat of fire from lightning, workshops and household hearths was constant. Most diseases were thought to be constant, making the close proximity of people all the more a source of fear.[12]

In just a few short years, the population of Geneva doubled from ten to twenty thousand due to immigration. Refugees from religious persecution overwhelmed the local population and turned "a tense situation in which political factionalism was rife into a powder keg."[13]

In this context of political tension, disease, and desperate need, Calvin commended the work of charity. He explained that acts of mercy were signs that Christians not only profess faith in a merciful God, but also serve that

God.[14] While Calvin stressed the special ties among brothers and sisters in the church—ties of solidarity in Christ that require wealthy believers to care for poorer believers—he preached that believers are bound to show mercy to *all* people. Deeds of charity and generosity to the poor characterize the life of holiness, while the neglect of the needy is a sacrilege. Preaching on Deuteronomy 15:11–15, he said:

> The one who shuts his ears to the cry of the poor shall cry himself and God will not hear. On the contrary, if we are compassionate (moved with pity) and, having heard of the destitution of the poor, are moved to help them, God also will bestow pity and have compassion on us to rescue us in a time of need. . . . God ordained that we should have an open hand to the poor who dwell among us. . . . Since our Lord gives us the means, we must not seek a subterfuge (we must no longer seek excuses), for we shall still remain guilty if we have not used the occasion that was offered to us.[15]

After spending three years in Strasbourg, Calvin returned to Geneva in 1541 and worked to make significant changes to church government. That year he wrote the Genevan Ecclesiastical Ordinances, a document meant to ensure the order and maintenance of the church by specifying four essential "offices instituted by our Savior for the government of his church": the offices of pastor, doctor, elder, and deacon. Pastors, doctors, and elders were charged with the proclamation of the word, instructing the faithful in sound doctrine, and promoting the spiritual vitality of the community. Yet these three offices were not enough. Sound doctrine and spiritual vitality could not be divorced from care for the poor, which was the special office of deacons.

According to Calvin, there were two kinds of deacons: "One has to receive, distribute, and care for the goods of the poor (i.e., daily alms as well as possessions, rents, and pensions); the other has to tend and look after the sick and administer the allowances to the poor as is customary." The sick, along with "old people no longer able to work, widows, orphans, children, and other poor people" were to be given particular attention in the city's hospital, whose officials should give special care to the poor scattered throughout the city. Calvin believed that the body of Christ could not function in a proper and orderly fashion without doing such work.

The labor of deacons was not easy. As Bruce Gordon writes,

> The deacons of the Genevan church did just about anything and everything. They purchased clothing and firewood, provided medical care, and not infrequently were present at births. They arranged guardians for the children of the sick. Essentially, they attempted to meet any need. Their task was thankless. The deacons had to respond immediately to whatever crisis landed at their doors—a sudden influx of refugees could arrive unannounced. They had to deal with difficult benefactors and recipients and the records are full of the ingratitude of those whom they helped, as well as the hostility of locals. People often stole the items they were loaned, and violent threats against the deacons were not uncommon.[16]

The task was immense and difficult, but the deacons were not alone: teachers, physicians, and others joined them. Calvin ensured that education was available to both boys and girls at a time when the latter were rarely schooled. He also put municipal resources to work in service to the poor. The city was to provide, at its own expense, a physician and surgeon for poor people in the hospital and all those in the city who were without means. Calvin was not only interested in helping those who had already fallen sick, but also in promoting public health, as evidenced by the fact that he helped to design a sanitation and sewer system for the city.[17] According to one historian, Calvin himself was the single greatest contributor to the *Bourse Francaise*, a fund specifically designated for the care of refugees through provision of apprenticeships, assistance with obtaining long-term employment, care of widows and orphans, and financing the reunion of refugee families by bringing in more immigrants from France.[18]

The ministry of mercy was not limited to deacons, for Calvin taught that all believers should put themselves and their resources in the service of their neighbors. Protestant ecclesiastical restructuring—especially the elimination of monasteries—required broader participation in care for the poor, and Protestant worship associated "almsgiving with the principal liturgy in a way new and different from either medieval or contemporary Roman Catholic worship."[19] Calvin and other preachers "repeatedly used the pulpit to remind the people of Geneva of their Christian duty towards those most vulnerable in society—the poor, the sick, the widowed and orphaned."[20] As Calvin wrote in a 1557 circular letter to the churches in Geneva, "Let us raise in *each* member of the Christian Community the spiritual problem of his material life, of his goods, of his time, and of his capabilities, in view of freely putting them at the service of God and neighbor."[21]

Thomas Chalmers

Three centuries after Calvin's ministry in Geneva, the Presbyterian clergyman and theologian Thomas Chalmers set another example for us in Glasgow, Scotland. As historian Mark Noll writes, "Chalmers' efforts while a minister in Glasgow to establish a new system of relief for the urban poor . . . made him the most widely noticed social reformer of his era." In particular, his treatise *The Christian and Civic Economy of Large Towns* became "probably the most widely read Christian response to the problems of industrialization ever published in English."[22] Chalmers was an influential minister of mercy during his lifetime, and since his death he has continued to inspire others to social concern and reform.

Chalmers became minister of Glasgow's Tron parish in 1815. Four years later, he became pastor to the parish of St. John's, which ministered to two thousand working-class families. The heads of households chiefly were employed as weavers and factory workers, and nearly all their children were uneducated. Chalmers saw education both as a central pursuit of the Christian life and as a key to improving the material welfare of the community. As one of his first acts of ministry at St. John's, Chalmers undertook the establishment of two schools that educated almost a thousand children at minimal cost to their families. For those too poor to afford even the smallest tuition bill, he opened Sabbath-schools—free, church-operated schools that provided Christian education. In a short time these Sabbath-schools enrolled more than twelve hundred children.

Chalmers also put the church to the task of meeting the material needs of the community. He divided his parish into twenty-five districts, appointing to each one a deacon charged with the care of material needs. The church took the lead in caring for the poor, collecting special offerings that were disbursed by elders as well as deacons. So great was the outpouring of mercy that within four years of beginning his ministry, the municipality's cost of care for the poor had decreased by 80 percent. This was accomplished in large part though Chalmers' "thorough organization of the parish . . . his personal visits among the poor and kindly sympathy with them, and his stimulation of the needy to self-respect and industry."[23]

Like Calvin, Chalmers emphasized both the obligation and the joy of participating in mercy ministry. He accentuated "the obligation which lies upon all of giving according to their means, either to relieve the want or help forward in any other way the well-being of their fellows." He also warned that lack of generosity toward the poor and needy was evidence of a practical atheism, of assuming that we, rather than God, are the creators, providers, and sustainers of our own wealth.[24] Chalmers' ministry was grounded in his theology, with his high regard for God's sovereignty and providence serving as the foundation of his intervention on behalf of the vulnerable.

According to Chalmers, Christians should consider themselves privileged to participate in the generosity of God, finding joy in benevolence. Yet they should resist the temptation to romanticize poverty or sentimentalize the work of charity. He wrote, "Benevolence is not merely a feeling but a principle—not a dream of rapture or fancy to indulge in, but a business for the hand to execute."[25] When Chalmers spoke of our own hands executing the business of benevolence, he had no room for distance from the poor, for simply funding the work of others:

> It is not enough that you give money, and add your
> name to the contributions of charity. You must give

it with judgment. You must give your time and your attention. You must descend to the trouble of examination. You must rise from the repose of contemplation, and make yourself acquainted with the object of your benevolent exercises.[26]

Personal involvement in the practical work of mercy ministry was fundamental to Chalmers' conception of mercy ministry.

Mercy Goes Global

Reformed approaches to mercy ministry are not merely historical artifacts. Many in the Calvinist tradition continue to leave their mark of mercy on the world. From contemporary global cities like New York to the farthest reaches of Africa, ministers of mercy continue to draw upon the rich theological resources of the Reformation.

Contemporary cities are marked by many of the same qualities that characterized Geneva and Glasgow. While the poorest of the poor are materially better off today, especially in the West—with lower infant mortality, longer life expectancy, and greater access to education than was the case in sixteenth-century Switzerland or nineteenth-century Scotland—the distance between the rich and the poor is at least as great today as it has ever been. In contemporary global cities, profound material suffering exists not merely alongside abundance, but alongside opulence. New York City is no exception. An exemplar of today's large cities, the Big Apple is both a cosmopolis—nearly every ethnic group is represented within its boundaries—and the world's premier global city. It is a site more or less directly articulated to global affairs, serving as a command and control center in the worldwide economy, a point of power in global politics, a node in international social networks, and a leader in cultural and cross-cultural affairs. At the same time, New York's share of local suffering is an immense burden.

In 1989, Timothy Keller founded New York's Redeemer Presbyterian Church, where one of the mottoes is "Seeking to renew the city socially, spiritually, and culturally." Keller's ministry has emphasized the role of Christian service and charity in the life of the church and its witness to the community. For this reason, Redeemer created a mission, Hope for New York, to partner with other nonprofit organizations that serve the poor and marginalized of New York City. Hope for New York (www.hfny.org) has since partnered with additional churches to organize volunteer and financial support for the poor in order to promote the social, economic, and spiritual well-being of individuals and communities as a demonstration of the love of God.

Hope for New York's range of ministry opportunities allows volunteers to use their gifts to help the poor. For example, songwriters and musicians in the congregation have collaborated to release recordings focused on the realities of urban life, the proceeds of which benefited Hope for New York. Professionals in Action, a skills-based volunteer program, helps congregants to put their legal, financial, and other vocational skills in the service of organizations that support the poor and marginalized.

Keller has often framed the call to Christian charity in ways that draw upon the work of America's greatest theologian, Jonathan Edwards. He writes, "I know of no better introduction to how the gospel moves us to minister to the poor than Jonathan Edwards' discourse 'Christian Charity.' Edwards concludes that giving to the poor is a crucial, nonoptional aspect of 'living out the gospel.' "[27] Like Calvin, Chalmers, and Edwards, Keller sees charity and mercy ministry as vital—not optional—functions of the body of Christ.

27

The Reformed tradition has inspired mercy ministry not only in Europe and the United States, but also in many places around the world. Christians from Africa to Asia to Latin America draw upon the doctrines of grace as they serve their neighbors. In 1991, various Reformed churches of Nigeria—led by the Reformed Church of Christ in Nigeria (RCCN) and the Evangelical Reformed Church of Christ in Nigeria (ERCC)—joined together to found the Reformed Ecumenical Council of Nigeria (RECON). RECON extends mercy ministry to the work of redressing the social causes of vulnerability and marginality by partnering to address needs arising from poverty, persecution, and violence. Programs emphasize community development, healthcare, literacy, medical care, and microfinance. The ERCC has also joined the Christian Rural Development Association of Nigeria, which promotes holistic education, community development, and capacity building through member organizations.

The work in Nigeria is just one example that illustrates a broader point: mercy ministry is for rural communities in developing countries as well as for influential cities in wealthy nations. Along with Reformed churches from Burkina Faso and Angola, RECON participates in the ACT Alliance, which works toward "positive and sustainable change in the lives of people affected by poverty and injustice through coordinated and effective humanitarian, development and advocacy work."[28] Through global partnerships, churches are administering mercy not only through charity toward the less fortunate, but also through programs meant to provide sustainable opportunities for everyone to flourish. By addressing corporate and structural aspects of sin and suffering, RECON and others are not only giving fish, so to speak, but teaching others to fish and ensuring access to the pond.

THE PRACTICE OF
MERCY MINISTRY

To this point, we have shown the biblical-theological warrant for mercy ministry and documented its historical scope. But how can we put this into practice? How can a church get started with its own ministries of mercy? As we seek to engage in this work, we do well to bear in mind a few practical tips, some of which are gleaned from our forebears in the faith.

At Least Give, But Don't Just Give

It is a common—and true enough—refrain: "Not everyone can go, but everyone can give." Without a doubt, it is important to give. Giving to provide for those in need is commended throughout Scripture. As James writes,

> If a brother or sister is poorly clothed and lacking in daily food, and one of you says to them, "Go in peace, be warmed and filled," without giving them the things needed for the body, what good is that? (James 2:15–16)

We are instructed to give both sacrificially and joyfully in imitation of Jesus Christ and as an expression of our faith in a sovereign God, who will put all things right in the end.

At the same time, we should not only give. Giving is not a substitute for the work of our hands. The key to Thomas Chalmers's ministry was not to find more money to distribute, but to recruit volunteers to "go out into the streets . . . to do the work of Christian ministry."[29] The closer we are to the situation, the better we understand the needs we seek to meet. Furthermore, the vulnerable need the blessing of friendship, which is not cultivated by staying at a distance writing a check.

We should follow the model set by Thomas Chalmers and find ways to involve ourselves personally in this work.

Individuals and congregations that volunteer to serve in mercy ministry can expect to receive as well as to give. There is spiritual blessing in the material support of others. We discover our own needs, even needs we had not previously known. We learn new things about God. And we are humbled as we learn from the people we serve. Few of these things happen through financial giving alone.

The effort to organize not only finances, but also volunteers, can build interest and develop a capacity for service in congregations that may be new to mercy ministry. As congregants catch the vision for serving God by serving their neighbors, they are inspired to deeper levels of commitment and more effective involvement.

Work Locally

One barrier to involvement in mercy ministry is the common impulse to go to the ends of the earth in search of opportunities. While we are called "to heal and to reveal"[30] to the ends of the earth, the desire to travel can be a barrier to local ministry. While it can be overwhelming—even paralyzing—to try to understand and address the needs of far-off communities, local alternatives allow us to do something, to start somewhere. We can always find significant opportunities for mercy ministry in our own neighborhoods or nearby cities. Often, the first momentum-building step toward effective ministry is to begin with the opportunities that God has provided close to home. Once we have built a platform for effective local mercy ministry—establishing congregational capacity through mobilization, communication, and finance—we can use that platform to reach across borders and minister to those who are far off.

It must also be said that our impulse to minister to the ends of the earth often emerges from an implicit exoticism. We find ourselves attracted to service opportunities that seem glamorous, sophisticated, or especially challenging, when we should also pay attention to the apparently banal suffering right around us. While we often find ourselves moved by the extraordinary suffering that gets attention in the headlines, we should also have compassion for the ordinary suffering in our immediate context.

Sometimes we are reluctant to serve locally because it is easy to think that needy people who are otherwise more or less like us must be suffering through some fault of their own and therefore hardly deserve our mercy. By contrast, it is easy to think that people whose circumstances are very different from our own are suffering on account of oppression and other injustices largely beyond their control. Focusing on those who are far off preserves for us the myth that those in situations like ours are solely responsible for their own misfortunes and, more perniciously, the myth that we are solely responsible for our fortunes.

But to serve local people, whose situations are more or less like ours, is to admit that God is free and we are not—that we are not able to explain, predict, and control our circumstances, and neither are the suffering poor. If our hearts cannot be moved by the suffering of those around us, then perhaps we ought to address our pride, hardness of heart, and inclination to disbelieve God' sovereignty, first with prayer and then with action that demonstrates the love of God even to those whose suffering may never make headlines.

Build Partnerships

Just as local opportunities can jumpstart mercy ministry by decreasing barriers to effectiveness and participation, partnership can do the same. Partner organizations that are involved in mercy ministry on an everyday basis can connect individuals and congregations with excellent opportunities for mercy ministry, effectively increasing the capacity of local organizations to achieve their ministry goals.

Many organizations are understaffed or lack professional expertise in specific niches. For example, community development organizations that provide basic medical care may not be able to employ medical professionals, but medical professionals may volunteer for them through partnerships. Other organizations exist for the express purpose of pooling resources and providing services that most congregations cannot. Hope for New York is one such organization, as it partners with churches like Redeemer Presbyterian Church to provide volunteer and financial resources to organizations that serve the poor and marginalized of New York City. Similarly, Administer Justice, which is located in the Chicago area, pools local legal talent to provide legal, educational, financial, and conflict resolution services for those in need.

It is important to note that partnerships not only benefit the organizations that are already working in mercy ministry, but also benefit the individuals and congregations that offer their talents and resources. Partnerships can teach us how to minister to human needs. We learn from partnership—even about the gospel. As Paul writes in his letter to the Romans,

> For I long to see you, that I may impart to you some spiritual gift to strengthen you—that is, that we may be mutually encouraged by each other's faith, both yours and mine. (Rom. 1:11–12)

Just as the apostle Paul looked forward to being encouraged by and learning from those to whom he ministered, so can we. Many Chicago-area churches partner with Mission USA and its BRIDGE program, which serves recovering addicts and people recently released from prison. Because of BRIDGE, Chicago churches can participate in mercy ministry without having to invent their own similar ministry. They can also learn about need from recovering addicts and paroled felons; in solidarity with them, the privileged may receive the blessing that God has given to the "poor, for [theirs] is the kingdom of God" (Luke 6:20).

Promote Justice

Finally, we should think carefully about mercy ministry that goes beyond the work of charity. The root causes of poverty, vulnerability, and marginality do not all lie within the individual, and therefore evangelism and charity are not the limits of our call. The results of the fall and its curse have affected our social structures, so that some are weighted in favor of the powerful and against the poor—a condition that God hates. But God has gifted some in the church with the talents and resources necessary to heal the sick, serve as a voice for the persecuted, and devise new opportunities for the marginalized. Whether through advocacy, microfinance, entrepreneurship, or other means, churches and individual Christians should seek opportunities to address root causes of poverty and other forms of human need.

THE CALL TO MERCY MINISTRY

This booklet began with the story of a homeless man on the doorstep of a Philadelphia church. There is more to that story. People from the church developed a friendship with the man, served him with loving deeds of mercy, and eventually were used by God to introduce him to Jesus Christ. Nor was he the only one, for in the following decades thousands of people were touched by the work of Active Compassion Through Service (ACTS), the mercy ministry of Philadelphia's Tenth Presbyterian Church (www.compassion.tenth .org). Some have become members of the congregation and have used their own gifts of mercy to serve the church and the city.

The same basic story plays out wherever people under the mercy of Christ extend his mercy to others. A need is noticed. The people of God respond in Christian love. They address the need with practical deeds of mercy. Hospitality replaces hostility as the stranger becomes a guest. The people of God proclaim the gospel, which is the greatest mercy of all, because only the good news of the cross and the empty tomb has the power to alleviate eternal suffering. A wound is healed. A life is restored. Relationships are reconciled.

Every believer in Christ is called to show such mercy. Our Savior intends for his saving work to find expression in our own servant ministry. This is Paul's point in Philippians 2, where he traces the trajectory of the Son of God from the courts of heaven down to the servant sufferings of the cross and then back up to the exaltation of his glorious and eternal throne. The apostle tells us this story to call us to ministry. Be mercy-minded, he says: "Let each of you look not only to his own interests, but also to the interests of others" (Phil. 2:4).

This command should lead to serious self-examination. Who is the recipient of my mercy? Is anyone's life being transformed by my compassion? Am I driven to show mercy to others, or am I dominated by my own pleasures and ambitions? Jesus said, "Blessed are the merciful, for they shall receive mercy" (Matt. 5:7). In all honesty, am I eligible to receive this blessing or not?

One of the best ways to test our grasp of God's mercy is to consider how we treat other sinners. How do we respond when we encounter a homeless person, or a drug addict, or a transsexual prostitute? How do we treat the person at work, at home, or at school who is the most difficult for us to love? Our usual response is to get angry and impatient and to wonder why some people never seem to get their act together. But this is hardly the response of someone who knows that the bondage of sin can only be broken through the mercy of the cross.

It is strange to say, but some Christians are Calvinists when they deal with their own sins, but Pelagians when it comes to the sins of other people. Although they have learned that the only possible solution for their sin is the grace of God, somehow they still expect other people to save themselves.

Certainly God holds people responsible for their sins, but he also reaches out to us in mercy. So we need to see again the mercy that we have been given in Christ. By his lowly birth and earthly poverty, Jesus totally identified himself with the poor. "At the end of his life," writes Timothy Keller, "he rode into Jerusalem on a borrowed donkey, spent his last evening in a borrowed room, and when he died, he was laid in a borrowed tomb. They cast lots for his only possession, his robe, for there on the cross he was stripped of everything."[31] Jesus suffered these degradations for us, impoverishing himself to enrich us with eternal life.

As we meditate on the merciful pattern of ministry that Jesus set for us in his servant life, sacrificial death, and saving resurrection, we see that the greatest motivation for giving to the poor is the gospel itself. Whatever feeble excuses we may have for avoiding mercy ministry are more than answered by our Savior's love. If we truly understand the grace that God has for us in the gospel, we will not be judgmental or proud, but we will become servants of his mercy.

NOTES

1 Jane Kenyon, *Otherwise: New and Selected Poems* (St. Paul, MN: Graywolf, 1996), 7.

2 Daniel L. Migliore, *Faith Seeking Understanding: An Introduction to Christian Theology*, 2nd ed. (Grand Rapids: Wm. B. Eerdmans Publishing Company, 2004), l2905.

3 Timothy Keller, "The Gospel and the Poor," *Themelios: An International Journal for Pastors and Students of Theological and Religious Studies*, 33, 3 (December 2008). Available at http://thegospelcoalition.org /publications/33-3/the-gospel-and-the-poor.

4 Migliore, *Faith Seeking Understanding*, l2539.

5 William M. Struthers, *Wired for Intimacy: How Pornography Hijacks the Male Brain* (Downers Grove, IL: 2009), 19–114.

6 Westminster Confession of Faith, Chapter 6: Of the Fall of Man, of Sin, and of the Punishment Thereof. See also Questions 20–29 in the Westminster Larger Catechism.

7 *Partners in Life: The Handicapped and the Church*, Geiko Müller-Fahrenholz, ed., World Council of Churches, Commission on Faith and Order, January 1, 1979, 32.

8 For more information about Harvest USA, visit its website, www .harvestusa.org.

9 John Calvin, quoted in Elsie Ann McKee, *Diakonia in the Classical Reformed Tradition and Today* (Grand Rapids: Eerdmans, 1989), 41. It is helpful to remember that, as McKee notes elsewhere, while *pietas* and *caritas* were inseparable for Calvin, he saw a clear logical sequence. Justification and worship precede and yet must be accompanied by regeneration and service. See idem., *John Calvin: On the Diaconate and Liturgical Almsgiving* (Travaux d'Humanisme et Renaissance 197) (Geneva: Librairie Droz, 1984).

10 Cited in John Piper, *A Godward Life: Savoring the Supremacy of God in All of Life* (Colorado Springs: Multnomah Books, 2001), 253.

11 Gregory of Nazianzus, cited in Stanley Hauerwas, "To Love God, the Poor, and Learning: Lessons Learned from Saint Gregory of Nazianzus," in *The State of the University: Academic Knowledges and the Knowledge of God* (New York: Blackwell, 2007).

12 Bruce Gordon, *Calvin* (New Haven and London: Yale University Press, 2009), 198.

13 Ibid.

14 Bonnie L. Pattison, *Poverty in the Theology of John Calvin* (Eugene, OR: Pickwick, 2006), 309–45.

15 Cited in Pattison, *Poverty in the Theology of John Calvin*, 324.

16 Gordon, *Calvin*, 201. See also Jeannine Olson, *Calvin and Social Welfare: Deacons and the Bourse Francaise* (Selinsgrove, PA: Susquehanna University Press, 1989).

17 William Stacy Johnson, *John Calvin: Reformer for the 21st Century* (Louisville: Westminster John Knox, 2009).

18 Olson, *Calvin and Social Welfare*.

19 McKee, *John Calvin: On the Diaconate*, 265.

20 Gordon, *Calvin*, 200.

21 John Calvin, quoted by Tom Skinner at the 1978 Association for Public Justice Conference hosted by Dordt College in Sioux Center, Iowa.

22 Mark Noll, "Thomas Chalmers (1780–1847) in North America (ca. 1830–1917)," *Church History* 66, 4 (December 1997): 762–77.

23 Ibid.

24 N. Masterson, ed., *Chalmers on Charity: A Selection of Passages and Scenes to Illustrate the Social Teaching and Practical Work of Thomas Chalmers* (Westminster: Archibald Constable and Company, 1900), 215.

25 Ibid., 221.

26 Ibid.

27 Keller, "The Gospel and the Poor." See Jonathan Edwards, "Christian Charity: or, The Duty of Charity to the Poor, Explained and Enforced," in *The Works of Jonathan Edwards*, rev. and corrected by Edward Hickman (1834; reprint, Carlisle, PA: Banner of Truth, 1974), 2:163–73; Timothy J. Keller, *Ministries of Mercy: The Call of the Jericho Road*, 2nd ed. (Phillipsburg, NJ: Presbyterian & Reformed, 1997).

28 "About Act Alliance," Act Alliance, accessed September 14, 2012, http://www.actalliance.org/about.

29 Mark Noll, "Thomas Chalmers (1780–1847) in North America," 770.

30 Richard Hays, *The Moral Vision of the New Testament: Community, Cross, New Creation: A Contemporary Introduction to New Testament Ethics* (San Francisco: HarperOne, 1996).

31 Timothy J. Keller, "The Gospel and the Poor."

MISSIONS RESOURCES FROM P&R

TIMOTHY J. KELLER

Ministries
of MERCY
THE CALL OF THE JERICHO ROAD

Timothy Keller demonstrates that caring for needy people is the job of every believer—not just church deacons—as fundamental to Christian living as evangelism, nurture, and worship. But Keller doesn't stop there. He shows how we can carry out this vital ministry as individuals, families, and churches.

Along the way, he deals perceptively with many thorny issues, such as the costs of meeting needs versus the limits of time and resources, giving material aid versus teaching responsibility, and meeting needs within the church versus those outside.

"*Ministries of Mercy* is a solid piece of work, the best of its kind that I have yet seen. It is concrete, down-to-earth, spelling out in specific detail every phase of what Keller calls the ministry of mercy."

—**Vernon C. Grounds**

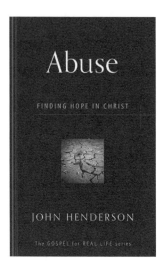